DATE DUE

The <u>most</u> <u>excellent</u> book of how to be a

puppeteer

Roger Lade

Illustrated by Rob Shone

Copper Beech Books
Brookfield, Connecticut

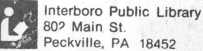

© Aladdin Books Ltd 1996
Designed and produced by
Aladdin Books Ltd
28 Percy Street, London
WIP 0LD

*First published in the
United States in 1996 by*
Copper Beech Books,
an imprint of
The Millbrook Press
2 Old New Milford Road
Brookfield, Connecticut
06804

Editor: Katie Roden
*Design:*David West
Children's Book Design
Designer: Edward Simkins
Illustrator: Rob Shone
All puppets made by
Roger Lade *except page
25* (David West)
All photography by Roger
Vlitos *except page 3 (top –*
Mary Evans Picture
Library; *middle, bottom –*
The Hutchinson Library)

Printed in Belgium

Library of Congress Cataloging-in-
Publication Data
Lade, Roger.
The most excellent book of how to be a
puppeteer / by Roger Lade. illustrated
by Rob Shone.
p. cm.
Includes index.
Summary: Describes how to make and
operate many types of puppets--from
sock and shadow puppets to
marionettes--and how to create puppet
theaters.
ISBN 0-7613-0526-2 (lib.bdg.). --
ISBN -07613-0505-X (pbk.)
1. Puppet theater--Juvenile literature.
2. Puppet theaters--Juvenile literature.
3. Puppet making--Juvenile literature.
[1. Puppet making. 2. Puppet theaters.]
I. Shone, Rob, ill. II. Title.
PN1972.L24 1996   96-12641
791.5'3--dc20   CIP AC

CONTENTS

INTRODUCTION

Puppets come from every corner of the world and in all kinds of styles. There are delicate Indonesian shadow and rod puppets *(bottom)* and beautiful Indian marionettes. Europeans enjoy the tradition of glove puppets, including the comedy of Punch and Judy *(right)*.

There are the spectacular fighting knights of the Sicilian Marionettes and the complex puppetry of the Bunraku Theater of Japan *(left)*. This book is an introduction to different types of puppets, how to make them, and how to use them.

As you read the book, look for these symbols:

★ shows the preparation you need to make before you create and perform with your puppets.

✔ will give you essential tips on how to perfect your craft as a puppeteer and things to remember as you perform.

Have fun with this book – and have fun with your puppets!

✔ *Choose some music to accompany your show, either recorded on tape or played live. Special effects can be created easily – for example, rustling potato chip bags can sound like crackling fire!*

Starting Out as a PUPPETEER

Writing Your Show

Start by making some puppets! Then you and your friends can each hold one or two puppets and play with the characters. Let the puppets chat together, move around, and get involved in everyday situations or fantastic adventures. Gradually you can invent stories together. Then write down a script, learn your parts, rehearse – and you'll be ready to perform a fantastic show!

Your Puppet Characters

Give your puppets very definite looks and characters so their actions and feelings are clear to the audience. Design the puppets first, so you have a good idea of what they should look like while you make and perform with them.

Keep It Focused!

To bring a puppet to life, you must always be aware of what it is looking at. Practice focusing the puppet's eyes on objects such as your finger. When you perform, the puppet will seem alive!

That's Entertainment!

Try to vary the pace of your show, to make it exciting for the audience. Fast moments can be followed by calmer episodes. Ask a friend to watch you rehearse.

Puppets for PRACTICE

The simplest puppets to make and operate.

Sad

Slit

★ *You will need: foam balls (from a toy store); glue; scissors; paper; colored markers; pieces of material.*

1 Take a foam ball and cut a slit into it with scissors.

2 Push your first finger into the slit.

3 Try out as many movements as you can. Experiment with different movements to show different emotions.

Angry

4 Stick on eyes, a nose, and a mouth in cut-out paper. Choose features that create the character suggested by some of the movements you have already made.

5 Practice with your puppet character, trying different hand actions. For example, clench your fist to show anger.

6 Try this with two puppets. Make them speak to each other.

Happy

Adding More Character

1 Make a hole in the material. Surround it with glue.
2 Push your finger through the hole and into the slit. The glue will make the scarf stick to the ball.
3 Decorate your puppet's head to give it a definite character!

Keep 'Em Up!

Glove puppets are usually used in a booth *(see pages 16-17)*. Practice holding them in the air at arm's length. Always look at the puppet that is speaking or moving; in this way, you will know exactly what it is doing.

✔ *Your hands must be flexible to operate your puppets. Keep them supple, without tension in the wrists or fingers. If your shoulders get uncomfortable, gently move your arms in a circular motion to ease the tension.*

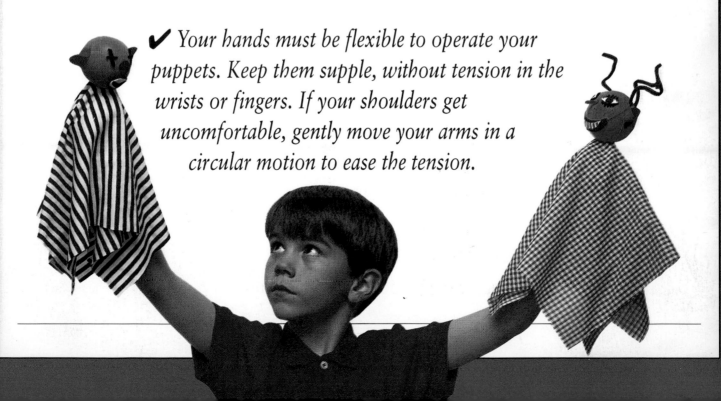

Basic GLOVE PUPPETS

Use this technique to invent your own characters.

★ *You will need: brown paper; water; clay; dowel; wallpaper paste; cardboard; paint; a bottle; material; a needle and thread; glue.*

1 Tear the paper into square pieces, about 1 inch across. Stir them into a bowl of warm water and leave for about 3 hours.

2 Put a lump of clay on the dowel. Hold it in one hand and sculpt it into a head and neck shape. Place it in the top of the bottle to keep it steady while you cover it.

3 Mix wallpaper paste with water until it is smooth but sticky.

4 Drain the water off the paper. Dip one piece at a time into the glue, then place it on the head. Keep sticking until it is covered firmly.

5 Mix a little paste with blue or red paint and rub it over the head, to show the finished layer.

6 Repeat steps 4 and 5 until you have made 4 layers of paper and paint.

7 Put the head in a warm place until all the layers are dry.

8 Ask an adult to cut the head in half lengthwise with a craft knife. Remove the clay and dowel then stick the head back together with more paper and glue. Allow it to dry.

9 Paint the head all over in one color. When this is dry, paint on a face. Use paper or cotton balls for hair and add accessories made from cardboard, such as a tall hat or a crown.

10 To make the costume, follow the pattern shown. Cut out two shapes and sew or glue the edges together. Leave the neck, sleeves, and skirt open.

11 Make hands from cardboard and paint them. Glue the hands and head to tubes of cardboard. Glue these into the sleeves and neck.

✔ For larger puppets, make a basic costume pattern then sew or glue a bigger version over the top. Put the hands and head on longer tubes of cardboard so your fingers can reach them.

The Dancing ROD PUPPET

This is based on a traditional Indonesian rod puppet.

★ *You will need: a half-gallon plastic milk container; a long cardboard tube; string; paper tape; strong cardboard; 2 gardening sticks; scissors; pieces of material; tissue paper; old jewelry; glue.*

1 Cut the bottom off the milk container. Save the leftover pieces – you'll need them later.

2 Fix a ring of cardboard onto the top of the tube. Push it into the neck of the container and secure it with tape.

3 Cut a large piece from the remaining plastic. Make a hole in it and put it over the top of the tube, to make shoulders. Secure it above and below with taped cardboard. Cut a small hole in each shoulder.

4 Cut out 4 thin strips of cardboard. For each arm, use 2 strips. Make a small hole in each end of the strips and tie them together with a piece of string, to make loose joints. Attach the arms to the shoulders with more pieces of string.

8 Hair

7 Face

1 Milk container

5 Cut hands from leftover plastic. Tie the wrists to the arms.

6 Cut 2 holes in each hand and loop a piece of string through. Fold it over the top of a stick and tape the ends.

7 Add a face to the milk container. Use the handle as a nose and add a painted mouth and paper eyes.

5
Plastic hands

6
String attachments

4
String joints

8 Scrunch up some tissue and stick it to the head.

9 Dress your puppet with material, jewelry, and other decorations. Make sure that the costume does not become too heavy, and think of how it will look when the puppet moves – it should not restrict the arms or head.

✔ *Hold the body tube in one hand and the arm rods in the other. Practice moving them in as natural a way as possible. Try inventing various characters in this way.*

The Rod Puppet MONSTER

A terrifying creature!!!

★ *You will need: 6 egg cartons; toilet paper tubes; cardboard; paper tape; glue; strong elastic; a knitting needle; 2 medium-sized boxes; garden wire; 2 gardening sticks; string; a small plastic ring; paints.*

1 Cut the egg cartons in half lengthwise, and glue together.
2 Measure the length of the boxes end-to-end. Cut a piece of elastic just over twice as long. Tape the elastic to the knitting needle and thread it through the boxes. Knot it in a loop.
3 Make each leg out of two tubes, jointed with string. Add cardboard feet. Attach the legs to the body with string.

4 Make a neck out of toilet paper tubes joined together with elastic. Make the tail using leftover pieces of egg cartons cut into pointed shapes, threaded on wire.

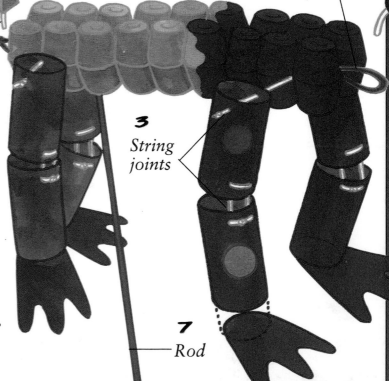

4

Wire

2 *Elastic*

3 *String joints*

7 *Rod*

5 To make the head, cut the boxes to make a jawlike shape. Tape them at the back so they open and close. Add cardboard features.

6 Decorate the puppet with brightly colored paints.

7 Attach the rods to the back carton and the lower jaw.

8 Cut string to go from the top of the head to the bottom of the front rod. Attach it to the back of the upper jaw. Make a hole in the neck and push the string through. Tie on the ring.

9 As you move your puppet, pull the string with your thumb to open and close the mouth.

✔ Make your monster speak using the techniques shown on page 7. Practice until you can move it smoothly and operate the mouth easily at the same time.

The Talking WIZARD

A lip-synch puppet with the gift of the gab!

★ *You will need: pieces of foam; colored felt; scraps of material; cardboard; costume material; needle and thread; glue; 2 gardening sticks; black paint.*

1 Cut the foam into the right shapes for a head, a lower jaw, ears, and a nose.

2 Cut out enough felt to cover the foam except the back of the head and jaw. Stick on the felt.

3 Cut 2 semi-circles of cardboard to fit inside the mouth. Glue them onto a circle of dark felt.

4 Glue the felt to the mouth to connect the head and jaw.

5 For a neck, stick felt into a tube.

6 Attach the neck to the back of the head.

Leave a hole so you can put your hand into the felt at the back of the head and move the mouth.

7 Cut felt shapes for the eyes and mouth. Glue them on.

8 Add hair, a beard, and a felt hat.

9 Highlight the features with paint.

10 Make a cone of material. Attach it to the neck.

11 Make each arm from 2 strips of felt taped to make a joint. Cover with cones of material and sew or glue them loosely to the robe.

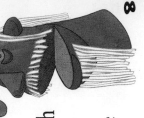

— **Tape joints**

12 Make hands from felt-covered cardboard. Tape them to the arms.

13 Attach the sticks in the same way as the rod puppets.

✔ To use the puppet, put one hand into the unglued felt so that you can move the mouth. Hold the rods in the other. Practice making the wizard speak. When you open your mouth, he should open his; when your mouth is shut, his should be, too. Try to make his movements match his emotions.

Glove and Rod Puppet BOOTHS

Colorful places to perform!

A Simple Booth For One Person

★ *You will need: some large, strong cardboard boxes; packing tape; paint and decorations.*

Playboard

1 Open the boxes and stick them together to make a three-sided booth that can stand up on its own. It should be tall enough so when you kneel down behind it you are invisible to the audience.

2 Stick more cardboard around the inside edge of the booth, to make a ledge. This is known as a "playboard" and is a place for the puppets to put props while they are performing.

3 Decorate your booth in bright, cheerful colors.

4 Kneel down and hold the puppets above your head.

A Theater For Several People

★ *You will need: 2 stable chairs; 2 brooms or long pieces of strong dowel; thumbtacks or strong tape; an old sheet; string; paints or decorations.*

Stand here.

❶ Position the chairs so that the backs are facing the direction of the audience.

❷ Tie one broom or piece of dowel to the outside edge of each chair. Make sure that the tops of the sticks are upright and level and that they are high enough to stand just above your head height.

❸ Attach the sheet to the tops of the poles with thumbtacks or tape.

❹ Pull the chairs apart until the sheet is taut.

❺ You can use the seats as places to rest any puppets that you are not using.

✔ *Always remember that the puppets should face outward, toward the audience. It is a good idea to ask a friend to watch you rehearse your show, so you know that everything can be seen. Don't lean on the sheet – your theater might fall over!*

Beautiful SHADOW PUPPETS

Create magical images and effects!

Black Shadows

★ *You will need: black cardboard of medium-thickness ; paper tape; gardening sticks; gardening wire; glue; string; paper; pens.*

Moving parts

1 Design a variety of puppet characters on a sheet of paper.

2 On the cardboard, draw each figure and all its separate moving parts, like arms and legs. Cut them out. Make sure no part is too narrow, as the puppet might get too floppy.

3 Mix a little glue with some water. Paint this onto each side of each puppet and let it dry, to make it stronger.

4 To attach the moving parts, make small holes with the tips of the scissors. Thread string through and knot it.

5 Make a loop of wire and tape it to the top of a stick. Tape the stick to the back of the puppet. Use one stick for each moving part.

Colored Shadows

★ *You will need: thin white cardboard; colored markers; a paintbrush; cooking oil; gardening wire; paper tape; string.*

1 Draw your puppets on the white cardboard. Color them in.

2 When they are dry, use the brush to cover them with a thin coating of cooking oil. This will make them more transparent. Allow them to dry.

3 Make the rods in a similar way as for the black puppets *(see page 18)*. However, to attach the sticks to the colored puppets, carefully make two small holes in each puppet then loop a short piece of string through. Tie or tape the ends around the wire loop on the stick.

✔ *Design puppets that tell a story for your show. Always store your puppets flat. Store the colored ones in wax paper so the oil does not stain furniture or clothes.*

Your SHADOW SCREEN

How to put on a stunning show!

★ *You will need: a large cardboard box; a sheet of white tracing paper or wax paper; glue; scissors; paint or pens; a bright desk lamp; tape.*

1 Cut the front off the box, leaving flaps at either side to help it stand up.

2 Cut a large, square hole in the front.

3 Stretch the paper over the hole, at the back of the screen. Make sure there are no wrinkles in it. Tape it firmly around the back of the hole.

4 Make two side flaps from some of the leftover cardboard. Glue or tape them to the screen so they stick out at the front.

5 Decorate your screen.

✔ *Stand the screen on a table (you could add a cloth). Place the lamp behind it so it points down onto the screen. Draw the curtains and turn off all other lights.*

1 Hold the puppets further back from the screen to make them look bigger – and scarier!

2 Hold the puppets close to the screen to produce clear shadows. Try using more than one with each hand.

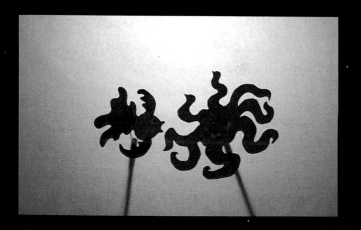

3 Always hold the colored puppets as close to the screen as possible.

4 Create hazy shadows by holding the puppets closer to the lamp.

A Knight in PLASTIC ARMOR

The most gallant of puppets!

★ *You will need: plastic cups and bottles; paints; glue; tape; string; corrugated cardboard; decorations (buttons, feathers, etc); a length of dowel; 4 screw eyes; gardening wire.*

1 Use an upside down plastic bottle as a head. Cut cups into features. Tape them to the bottle.

2 Use another bottle, upside down, for the body. For a chest, cut and glue another bottle.

3 Make a hole in the top of the shoulders. Push string through and knot an end. Make a hole in a piece of cardboard. Push the other end of the string into it and knot it. Roll the cardboard up. Push it into the neck.

4 Cut down various cups to make hips and shoulders. Tape them to the body.

String joints

Measure the height of its head, shoulders, hands, and knees.

10 Hold your arm out at waist height. Measure this height.

11 Subtract the puppet's measurements from the height of your outstretched arm to find the length of the strings.

12 Measure out your strings, but double the length.

13 Ask an adult to attach the eyes to the dowel.

14 Loop the strings through the eyes. Tape the strings to the head, knees, shoulders, and hands as shown.

15 Hang up the puppet then paint and decorate it.

Screw eyes

14

String joints

7

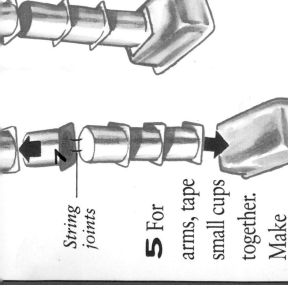

5 For arms, tape small cups together. Make elbow joints by knotting string through the fronts of the cups.

6 Make hands and a sword from cut down cups.

7 Make the legs in the same way as the arms, and feet from tubs. Make knee joints by knotting string through the backs of the cups.

8 Loosely attach the arms to the shoulders with string, and the legs to the hips.

9 Stand the puppet upright.

The Friendly GHOST

...but he'd really like to be scary!

★ *You will need: an elasticized fabric; cotton balls; rope; a needle and thread; muslin; glue; 2 dowels; 6 screw eyes; string; paint; buttons.*

1 Sew or glue a length of fabric into a tube. Stuff it with cotton balls to make 3 sausage shapes. Leave another section unstuffed to make a neck. Sew up the ends of each "sausage."

Leave neck unstuffed

Rope arms **4**

2 Make features on the face by stitching or gluing the fabric. Add the buttons for eyes and outline the features with paint.

3 Make hands by sewing fabric.

4 Cut 2 lengths of rope for arms. Sew or glue on the hands, then sew or glue them to the shoulders.

5 Cut two ragged squares of muslin. Sew or glue one to the body and arms and the other to the lower body.

6 Tape the dowels together. Ask an adult to attach the eyes, then loop on the strings as shown. Knot the ends. Sew the knots to the hands, head, and the back two "sausages."

The PIED PIPER

A tuneful puppet!

★ *You will need: straws; a Ping-Pong ball; string; glue; a toilet paper tube; paint; clay; paper; wool; a piece of wire; fabric.*

1 Cover the tube with paper clothes.

2 Push one end of the wire into the ball and the other through the back of the tube. Hold it there with clay.

3 To make arms and legs, cut 4 straws in half and thread string through. Make holes in the tube and tie on the strings. Add paper hands, feet, and a pipe. Add clay to the feet.

4 Draw on a face. Add a paper nose and hat, wool hair, and a cloak.

5 Cross and tape two straws, then tie on strings as shown.

✔ To fly the ghost, hold the control horizontally and swoop him through the air, so his robe flaps behind him.

Using MARIONETTES

Bring your puppet characters to life!

1 Make sure you are holding the puppet at a comfortable height.

2 Always watch the puppet.

3 To move a part of the puppet, pull only one side of the string, holding the control with the other hand.

4 Try wiggling the control to see what other effects you can make.

5 If you are making a marionette walk, keep its feet in contact with the ground. Move it with a bouncy step.

6 Contrast is very important in puppetry. Emphasize the features of each puppet, such as the knight's heavy feet or the ghost's lightness.

Your MARIONETTE STAGE

A place to put on a perfect performance!

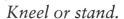

Kneel or stand.

★ *You will need: strong chairs; an old sheet; clothespins; paint, felt, or other decorations.*

1 Put the chairs in a line, with their backs facing toward where the audience will be.
2 Decorate your sheet to suit your show, then drape it over the backs of the chairs. Secure it with clothespins if necessary.
3 Kneel or stand on the chairs and hold the puppets over the chair backs.

✔ *To be unseen, put one more chair on each side of the stage. Tie on brooms or a dowel to a height at which your head will be covered while you perform. Drape a sheet between them.*

The BUNRAKU MAN

An ancient Japanese puppetry tradition.

★ *You will need: several long cardboard tubes; brown cardboard; thin dowel; packing tape; 2 gardening sticks; tape; thin elastic; glue; black paint or ink.*

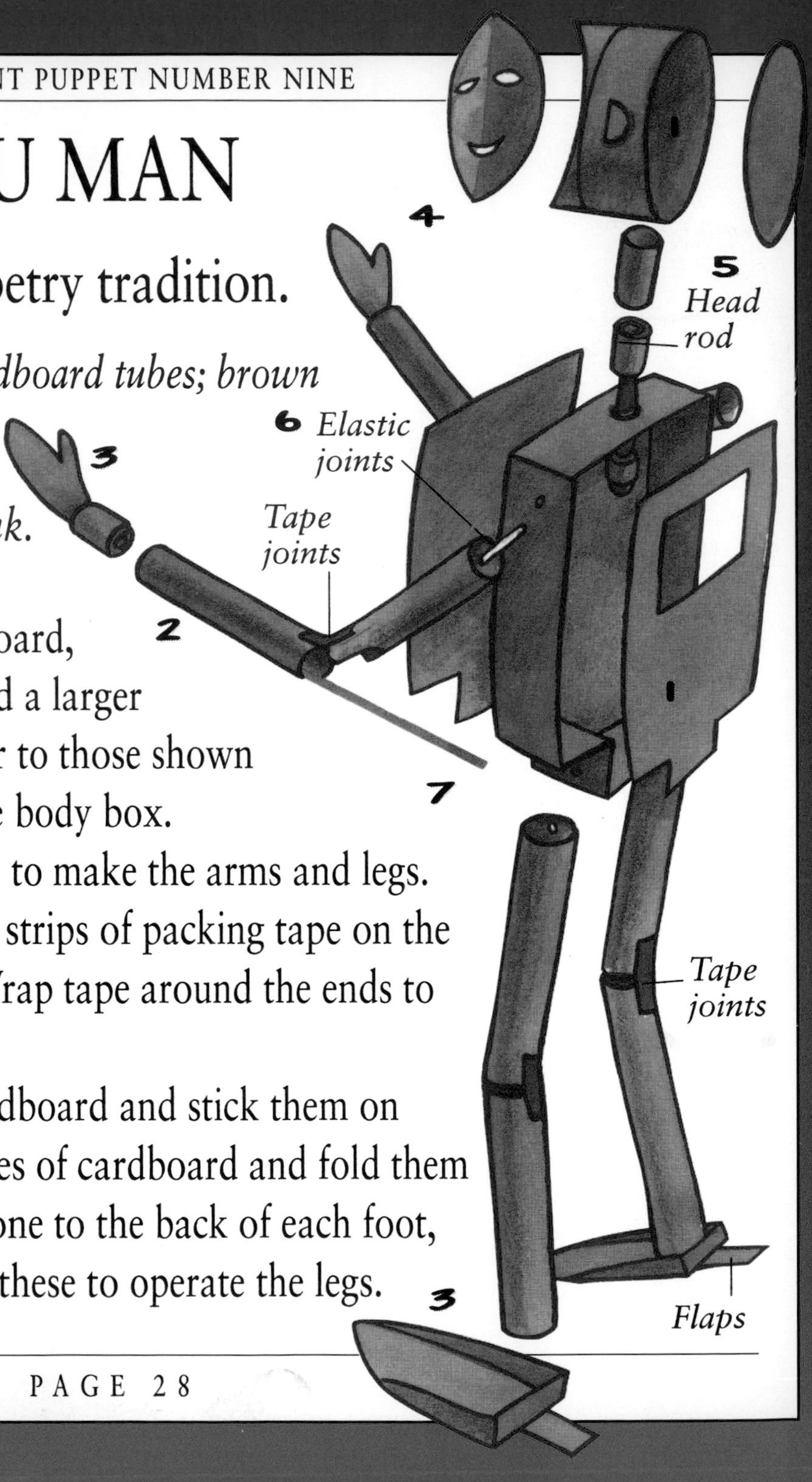

1 By cutting and taping the cardboard, make a small box for the head and a larger one for the body, in shapes similar to those shown here. Cut a hole in the back of the body box.

2 Use cut down cardboard tubes to make the arms and legs. Make knee and elbow joints with strips of packing tape on the inside and outside of the tubes. Wrap tape around the ends to give the joints extra strength.

3 Make hands and feet from cardboard and stick them on with tape. Cut out two small pieces of cardboard and fold them over to give them strength. Stick one to the back of each foot, to make small flaps. You will use these to operate the legs.

4

3

2

5 Head rod

6 Elastic joints

Tape joints

7

Tape joints

3

Flaps

4 Make the face from a piece of cardboard. Cut eye and mouth holes, and glue on shaped features. Glue the face to the head box.

5 Use the dowel for a neck. Put a tube over it. Attach it to the body the head. Stick a small ring of cardboard to each end to hold it in place. The head is operated by moving the dowel through the back hole.

6 Loosely attach the legs and arms by knotting elastic through the cardboard.

7 Tape one gardening stick firmly into the lower tube of each arm. These are used for movement.

✔ *If you give your puppet a costume, use light material so it can move easily. Make sure the arm and head rods and the feet flaps are not covered. This is a puppet for three people, but you could make one for even more operators.*

Using your BUNRAKU-STYLE PUPPET

So simple... but so effective!

Three people are needed to hold and operate this puppet:

I **Puppeteer One** holds the head rod in his or her left hand and the right arm rod in the right hand.

2 **Puppeteer Two** holds the feet flaps.

3 **Puppeteer Three** works the left arm.

4 Operate your puppet on an ordinary tabletop. Cover it with a sheet or cloth for decoration.

5 You will be in view all the time, so wear the same color clothes. Puppeteers often wear black, to be a bit less visible.

6 It is important that the audience watch the puppet and not you! This can be achieved if you always look at the puppet as you operate it. Keep your faces calm – silly or exaggerated expressions can be very distracting for the audience!

7 Practice moving your puppet around the table. Puppeteer One should always lead the puppet by moving its head. This makes the puppet look as if it is thinking before it moves. Keep the movements smooth and controlled. See how much expression you can put into the puppet's actions; try to match them to its emotions.

Watch the puppet – not the audience!

✔ *If you want your puppet to speak, Puppeteer One should provide a voice for it. If you give your puppet a costume, use clothing and accessories which emphasize the character that you have chosen for it.*

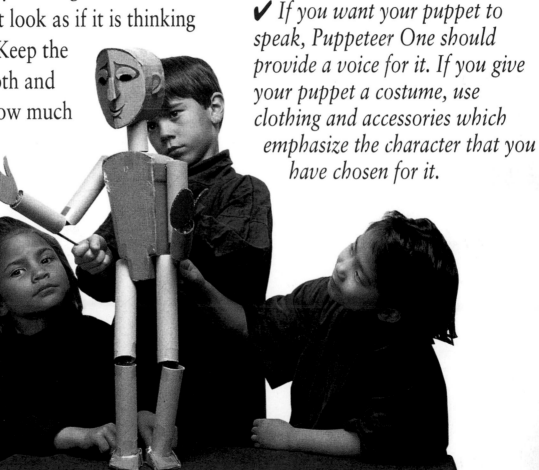

Puppet WORDS

Audience The people who come to watch your show.
Character The way in which a puppet behaves.
Focus To look constantly at one place or object.

Lip-synch A puppet with a movable mouth.
Marionette A puppet that is controlled by strings.
Props All the objects you use during your show.
Rehearsing Another word for practicing.
Script All the words and actions that the puppets perform during a show.

More Puppetry IDEAS

Invent new puppets! Keep a notebook of your ideas. All the techniques shown in this book can be combined and used for other puppets. Keep practicing... and keep on having fun!

INDEX